THE BROKEN JUG

HEINRICH von KLEIST

THE
BROKEN JUG

A Comedy

Translated from the German
and with an introduction by

JOHN T. KRUMPELMANN

Professor of German
Louisiana State University

FREDERICK UNGAR PUBLISHING CO.
NEW YORK

92571

Translation first published 1939
Copyright 1939 by Poet Lore

Revised version 1962

Copyright © 1962 by Frederick Ungar Publishing Co., Inc.

Printed in the United States of America

Library of Congress Catalog Card No. 62-9684

INTRODUCTION

Bernd Wilhelm Heinrich von Kleist was born in Frankfurt-on-the-Oder October 18, 1777, the scion of a family long prominent in German literature and Prussian military affairs. Possessed of a powerful dramatic genius, but handicapped by a sickly body and an erratic, morose, morbid spirit, he spent his short life in wandering from place to place and shifting from one career to another. Finding peace and satisfaction nowhere, constantly oppressed by pecuniary need, and finally broken in mind and spirit by the humiliation which his fatherland was suffering under the domination of the Napoleonic regime, this patriotic poet found death by his own hand at Wannsee, near Berlin, on November 21, 1811.

A cadet in the Potsdam Guard Regiment at the age of fourteen, he obtained his release as a lieutenant in 1798, returned to his native town, entered its university and devoted himself to the study of mathematics, philosophy and political science. Here he became engaged to Wilhelmine von Zenge.

In 1800 he went to Berlin to enter the civil service, but, after a trip to Würzburg in search of physical health, his restless spirit impelled him to change his plans and set out for Paris to continue his studies. Coming under the influence of the teachings of Rousseau, he went to Switzerland intent upon purchasing a small estate and settling down to a quiet rustic existence. Since Wilhelmine was not in sympathy with his dream of peasant simplicity their engagement lapsed. Already (1802) Kleist declares that his only wish is to die.

In Switzerland he completed *The Feud of the Schroffensteins* (see *Poet Lore*, Vol. 27, 1916) a fate-drama, and began his comedy *The Broken Jug*. After serious illness he returned

v

to Germany and spent some time in the vicinity of Weimar, where he visited Goethe, Schiller and Wieland.

In 1803 we find him in Dresden, whence he soon set out on a trip which led him through Switzerland and upper Italy to Paris. He failed to find solace in travel. Depressed and disappointed he burned all his manuscripts and pondered suicide. After another long spell of illness in Mayence he returned to his native Prussia (June, 1804).

From this time till 1807 he enjoyed comparative peace in Königsberg, where he held a minor position in the civil service and pursued his literary plans. He completed *The Broken Jug;* wrote his *Amphitryon,* based on a work of Molière, and busied himself with other dramas and short stories, among the latter his best-known, *Michael Kohlhaas.*

In January, 1807, he was arrested by the French in Berlin, charged with espionage and held prisoner in French fortresses until the end of July. Upon his release he settled in Dresden where he lived among congenial friends until 1810. During this period of fruitful literary activity he edited the *Phöbus,* a periodical dedicated to the arts, (1808-1809), completed his powerful Amazonian drama *Penthesilea* (1807); a romantic drama of chivalry, *Kathie of Heilbroun* (1808) and the patriotic drama, the *Hermannschlacht* (1808).

In January, 1810, he took up his residence in Berlin. Here he founded a political periodical, the *Berliner Abendblätter,* which survived only six months. Here he wrote his masterpiece *Prinz Friedrich von Homburg* (1810), a patriotic drama, which became one of the most popular pieces on the German stage. But even this failed to gain recognition for him. His courage broken, his financial resources exhausted, sick at heart and in mind, he sought in death that rest which he had not found in life.

The approbation which was denied the living Kleist has since been bestowed upon his memory. He is now universally acknowledged to be one of the greatest German dramatists. His short stories are widely read and admired. His *Broken Jug* must be included in any mention of the five or six best German comedies.

Ironical as it may seem, the first presentation of this comedy resulted in one of Kleist's bitterest disappointments. On March 2, 1808 *The Broken Jug* was produced as "a comedy in three acts" in the Weimar Theater under the direction of Goethe. It was a complete failure. That Goethe was in part the innocent cause of this failure cannot be gainsaid. But Kleist became exceedingly bitter and charged that Goethe had purposely caused the fiasco.

It was in Hamburg in 1820 that *The Broken Jug* began its successful parade across the German stage. It is still today, and will probably long continue to be, one of the all too few excellent comedies in German literature.

American readers who wish to learn more about this comedy and the dramatic genius of its author would do well to make the acquaintance of the very readable and dependable volume of Professor John C. Blankenagel, *The Dramas of Heinrich von Kleist* (1931).

Kleist's *Der zerbrochene Krug*, his only unequivocal comedy, is realistic, coarse and individualistic. Although the subject is said to have been inspired by a painting by Louis Philibert Debucourt from an engraving by Jean Jacques LeVeau, *Le Juge, ou la cruche cassée* (*The Judge, or the Broken Jug*), the milieu of the comedy, whose setting is in a Dutch village, seems to represent the spirit expressed in the genre paintings of Teniers, of Breughel or Ostade. The comedy anticipates modern realism, being a drama of social import. If Kleist's work portrays a psychological process, its psychology is not pathological but robust. Its import is not didactic.

Adam, the protagonist, is an individualist and Frau Martha, who plays opposite him, represents an honest, unpolished low-German peasant woman.

The plan of the comedy seems to have been conceived in Switzerland in February, 1802. The first three scenes were dictated in Dresden a year later. Early in 1805 work continued in Berlin, in the summer of which year the manuscript was sent to Dresden. In July, 1807 it was recommended to Goethe, under whose direction it was staged in Weimar on March 2,

1808. It proved a colossal failure, due evidently not to any shortcomings of the comedy itself, but to the inadequacy of the director. This debacle resulted in a never-to-be-healed breach between the sage of Weimar and the "Torch of Prussia." The drama was subsequently rejected by Iffland, the theater director in Berlin. Not until 1811 could Kleist find a publisher for what has come to be considered "along with Lessing's *Minna von Barnhelm* (1767) and Freytag's *The Journalists* (1852) the best German comedy." (Gundolf, p. 61).

The interest in the *Krug* centers not in the situation but in the characters. In fact, all the dramatic action in the plot represents no more then the disclosing of action which has taken place before the curtain rises. What is revealed on the stage is a display of mental cunning in a battle of wits between the characters as the complication caused by the preceding action is unravelled. The whole Aristophanian comedy is but the *dénouement* of a regular classical drama. Just as Shakespeare's Falstaff is a character *sui generis* at the royal court of England, so is Adam a similar character at the law court of a village in the Dutch Netherlands. As in Shakespeare, so here the scintillating language is that of the author rather than of the characters.

THE BROKEN JUG

CHARACTERS

WALTER, district judge
ADAM, village judge
LIGHT, clerk of court
MRS. MARTHA RULL
EVE, her daughter
VEIT DIMPEL, a peasant
RUPRECHT, his son
MRS. BRIDGET
A servant, bailiffs, maids, etc.

The action takes place in a village in the Netherlands, near
    Utrecht.
Scene: The Courtroom

SCENE 1

Adam is sitting and bandaging his leg.

Light enters.

LIGHT: Oh, what the deuce! Come tell me, brother Adam!
  What has befallen you? How you do look!
ADAM: Yes, look. To stumble one needs naught but feet.
  On this smooth floor here is there any stump?
  Yet I have stumbled here; for each one bears
  A cursed stumbling block within himself.
LIGHT: No, tell me friend! Each one bears such a block—?
ADAM: Yes, in himself!
LIGHT: Oh, cursed be that!
ADAM: What then?
LIGHT: Your family-tree sprouts from a fallen forebear,
  Who at the very start of all things fell,   10
  And through his fall has made himself quite famous.
  But you have not—?
ADAM: Well?
LIGHT: Likewise—?
ADAM: If I—? I think—?
  I fell down here. That's what I'm telling you.
LIGHT: Not actually crashed down?
ADAM: Yes, actually.
  It must have been an ugly act to see.
LIGHT: And when did this misfortune come to pass?
ADAM: Just at this moment, as from out of bed
  I climbed. My morning song was still upon
  My lips, when into morning I did trip,

3

And ere I could begin the day's swift course,   20
Our Lord above caused me to sprain my foot.
LIGHT: And then the left one too to boot?
ADAM: The left one?
LIGHT: This staid one here?
ADAM: Of course!
LIGHT: All-righteous Lord!
The one that found the way of sin hard walking?
ADAM: That foot! What? Hard? Why, why?
LIGHT: The clubfoot?
ADAM: Clubfoot!
Each foot, like every other, is a clump.
LIGHT: Oh please! Therein you do your right foot wrong.
The right foot cannot boast of this—great weight
And sooner dares to tread upon thin ice.
ADAM: Go on!
Where this one dares to go the other follows.   30
LIGHT: And what has put your face so out of joint?
ADAM: My what? My face?
LIGHT: What? You know nothing of it?
ADAM: I'd have to be a liar.—How does it look?
LIGHT: How does it look?
ADAM: Yes, dear old pal.
LIGHT: Most dreadful!
ADAM: Explain yourself more clearly.
LIGHT: The skin's all off.
A loathsome sight. A piece of cheek is missing.
How big? I'd need a scale to learn its weight.
ADAM: The devil then!
LIGHT (brings a mirror): Here. Now convince yourself!
A sheep, that, set upon by dogs, breaks through
A hedge of thorns, leaves no more wool ahanging   40
Than you have lost in skin, the Lord knows where.
ADAM: Hm! Yes! 'Tis true. It's not a lovely sight.
My nose has suffered also.
LIGHT: And your eye.
ADAM: But not my eye, old fellow.

LIGHT: Oh, here lies
  Right 'cross it a bloody blow, so help me God,
  As if a peasant foreman had struck in rage.
ADAM: That is the bone around my eye.—Just look.
  And yet I hadn't even felt all that.
LIGHT: Yes, yes! It goes thus in the heat of battle.
ADAM: Of battle! What? With that accursed goat's head   50
  Atop the stove I fought, if you so will. Now I recall.
  When I had lost my balance, and like one drunk,
  I grasped in vacant space around, about me,
  I caught my trousers, which the night before
  I'd hung all wet there on the stove-encasement.
  You understand. I grab them and I hope
  To brace my foolish self on them, and now
  The belt-band breaks, and band and pants and I
  Crash headlong and I smash my forehead straight
  Against the stove just where the billy-goat   60
  Sticks forth his head to ornament the corner.
LIGHT (laughs): Fine! Fine!
ADAM: Be damned!
LIGHT: You've fallen as Adam did,
  But now's the first time it's been from a bed.
ADAM: My Soul! But what I wished to say: "What's news?"
LIGHT: Yes, what's the news! The devil take it all!
  I'd mighty near forgot it.
ADAM: Well?
LIGHT: Make ready now for a quite unexpected
  Visit from Utrecht.
ADAM: What?
LIGHT: The district judge is coming.
ADAM: Who's coming?
LIGHT: Walter, the district judge, he comes
  From Utrecht.
  He's making an inspection tour of all the courts.   70
  This very day he comes to us.
ADAM: This day! Have you gone mad?
LIGHT: As sure as life.

He was in Holla, the border village, yesterday.
The court of justice there he has inspected.
A peasant saw a team of fresh, fine horses
Hitched to the coach to make the trip to Huisum.

ADAM: This very day the district judge from Utrecht!
The honest man, who knows how to fleece his lambs,
Hates all such monkey-shines at the inspection.
To come to Huisum and to bother us!   80

LIGHT: If he came to Holla, he'll also come to Huisum.
Be careful then!

ADAM: Go on!

LIGHT: I'm telling you!

ADAM: Away with fairy-tales I've told you once.

LIGHT: The peasant himself has seen him, damn it all!

ADAM: Who knows whom the bleary-eyed old scamp has seen?
Those rascals cannot tell a human face
From the back of a head, if only the latter's bald.
Just set a hat, three-cornered, atop my cane,
And hang a cloak around it, two boots beneath,
Then such a louse will take it for whom you will.   90

LIGHT: All right, go on and doubt, in the devil's name,
Until he enters at your door!

ADAM: He enter!—
Without one single word sent in advance.

LIGHT: Such ignorance! As if the former inspector,
The Counsellor Juniper, were still in office!
It's Counsellor Walter who holds the inspection now.

ADAM: What if it's Counsellor Walter. Leave me in peace!
Of course the man has sworn his oath of office,
And practices, as we, according to
The edicts and the customs now prevailing.   100

LIGHT: Well, I assure you, District Justice Walter
Appeared in Holla yesterday, unexpected,
Examined the accounts and records there
And then suspended the justice and his clerk.
For what? I know not, *ab officio*.

ADAM: The devil! What? Did the peasant tell you that?

LIGHT: That and still more—

ADAM: So?

LIGHT: If you care to know it,
This morning early, when they sought the judge,
Who had been ordered not to leave his quarters,
'Twas 'way back in the barn they finally found him. 110
Close to the roof he dangled from a rafter.

ADAM: What's that you say?

LIGHT: The meanwhile help arrives.
They cut him down, rub him, sprinkle him,
Yet they can barely bring him back to life.

ADAM: What? Do they bring him?

LIGHT: And now his house is sealed,
An inventory sworn, his doors are locked.
It is as if he were a corpse already.
His very rank as judge has been inherited.

ADAM: Oh hell! You see! A careless cur he was—
But yet an honest dog, as sure as I live, 120
A guy with whom a fellow liked to be.
But fearfully dissolute, I must say that.
If the inspector was this day in Holla,
Then I'll believe the poor old duck fared ill.

LIGHT: 'Twas this affair alone, the peasant said,
That kept the inspector from being here already.
By noon, he said, he'd be here without fail.

ADAM: By midday! Good! Old boy! Now show your friendship!
You know, of course, one hand can wash the other.
I know you yearn to be a village judge. 130
And you deserve it, by heavens, as well as any.
Today is not your opportunity.
Just let this chalice pass us by today.

LIGHT: Town-justice, I! What do you take me for?

ADAM: You are a friend of well-composed oration.
Your Cicero you've studied just as well
As any one in school in Amsterdam.
Suppress ambition just today; you hear?
Still other cases will sure present themselves

Where you will have a chance to show your skill.   140
LIGHT: We two old cronies! Away with such bad thoughts!
ADAM: In his good time the great Demosthenes
  Kept silent. Just take him now as your model.
  And though I'm not the King of Macedon,
  I can be grateful in my little way.
LIGHT: Away with your suspicion, I have said.
  Have ever I—?
ADAM: See, I, I, for my part
  Do follow too the great Greek as my model.
  Concerning public monies and interest yields
  A great oration might at length be wrought: 150
  But who should care to coin such sentences?
LIGHT: Well then!
ADAM: From such reproach I am quite free,
  The devil take it! And all that it concerns
  Is nothing but a prank which, born at night,
  Now shuns the daylight's prying ray.
LIGHT: I know.
ADAM: My soul! There is no reason why a judge,
  When he's not sitting in the Chair of Justice,
  Should be as solemn as a polar bear.
LIGHT: I'll say so too.
ADAM: Well then, come here, old pal.
  Just follow me into the record-room.   160
  The heaps of documents I'll set in order.
  They lie there like the very tower of Babel.

SCENE 2

A Manservant enters. The former characters.

Afterwards, two maids.

MANSERVANT: God bless you, judge! The District Justice Walter
  Sends you his greetings. He'll be here anon.

ADAM: Oh, most gracious Heavens! Is he already
    Finished in Holla?
MANSERVANT: Yes, he's in Huisum now.
ADAM: Hey! Liza! Maggie!
LIGHT: Quiet, quiet now!
ADAM: My dear old fellow!
LIGHT: Send back your thanks to him.
MANSERVANT: Tomorrow he departs for Husahe.
ADAM: What shall I do? What shall I do?   170

(He reaches for his clothes.)

FIRST MAIDSERVANT *(enters)*:   Sir, I'm here.
LIGHT: Will you put on your pants? Have you gone mad?
SECOND MAIDSERVANT *(enters)*: I'm here, Sir Village Judge.
LIGHT: Now take your coat.
ADAM *(looks around)*: Who? The District Judge?
LIGHT: Oh, it's the maid.
ADAM: My bands! My coat! My collar!
FIRST MAIDSERVANT: But first your vest.
ADAM: What? Coat off! Quick.
LIGHT *(to the Manservant)*: Our District Judge will be
    Indeed quite welcome here. We are prepared
    To greet him instantly. Go, tell him that.
ADAM: The devil, then! The Justice, Adam, begs
    To be excused.
LIGHT: To be excused!
ADAM: Excused.
    Is he perhaps already on the way?   180
MANSERVANT: He's in the tavern still. He has called the smith.
    Our coach has broken asunder.
ADAM: Fine. My respects.
    The smith is slow. I beg to be excused.
    Say I have almost broken my neck and legs.
    Just see yourself! A spectacle to behold!
    And every fright effects a natural purge.
    Say I am sick.

LIGHT: What? Have you lost your mind?
  The District Judge should be quite welcome here.
  You wish—?
ADAM: The devil!
LIGHT: What?
ADAM: The devil take me,   190
  If it's not just as if I'd taken a physic!
LIGHT: But still you need not light the way for him.
ADAM: Hey! Marguerite, you bag-of-bones! Oh, Liza!
THE TWO MAIDSERVANTS: We're here. What is your wish?
ADAM: Away! I say.
  Go take the cream-cheese, butter, ham and sausages
  And bottles from the record-room! And quick!
  Not you. The other girl.—You gaping ape, you.
  Good Heavens, Marguerite! The cow-maid, Liza, shall go
  Into the record-room! (*The first maid goes out.*)
SECOND MAID: Speak, if one's to understand you!
ADAM: Shut up, I say! Be gone! And fetch my wig!
  Quick, From the bookcase! Hurry! Get along!   200

  (*The second maid goes out.*)

LIGHT (*to the Manservant*): The District Judge, I hope, has not
    encountered
  Aught of ill luck upon his journey here?
MANSERVANT: Our carriage was turned over in a hollow.
ADAM: Plague! My skinned foot! I cannot get my shoes—
LIGHT: Oh my! Great Heavens! Overturned, you say?
  But no further damage?
MANSERVANT: None of importance.
  My master sprained his hand; but just a little.
  The coach-shaft broke.
ADAM: I wish he'd broken his neck!
LIGHT: He sprained his hand! Good Lord! And did the smith
    come?
MANSERVANT: Yes, for the shaft-pole.
LIGHT: What?

ADAM: You mean the doctor. 210
LIGHT: What?
MANSERVANT: For the shaft-pole?
ADAM: Oh no! For the hand.
MANSERVANT: Adieu, dear Sirs.—I think the blokes are mad. (*Exit.*)
LIGHT: I meant the smith.
ADAM: You give yourself away, old boy.
LIGHT: How so?
ADAM: You are perplexed.
LIGHT: What?

(*The first maid enters.*)

ADAM: Hey, Liza!
   What have you there?
FIRST MAID: It's Brunswick sausage, Judge!
ADAM: Those are the guardians' records.
LIGHT: I, perplexed!
ADAM: They go back to the record-room again.
FIRST MAID: The sausages?
ADAM: No! The papers they are wrapped in.
LIGHT: That was a misunderstanding.
THE SECOND MAID (*enters*):   In your book case,
   Sir Judge, I cannot find your periwig.   220
ADAM: Why not?
SECOND MAID: Hm! 'cause you—
ADAM: Well?
SECOND MAID: Yesterday evening—
   At 'leven—
ADAM: Well? Shall I hear it?
SECOND MAID: Oh you, you came
   Back home, just think it over, without your wig.
ADAM: I, without my periwig?
SECOND MAID: Indeed.
   There stands Eliza who can bear me witness.
   And your other one is at the periwig-maker's.
ADAM: Could I—?

FIRST MAID: Yes, 'pon my word, Sir Justice Adam!
  You were baldheaded when you came back home;
  You said that you had fallen; don't you know?
  I had to wash the blood from off your head.   230
ADAM: The shameless hag!
FIRST MAID: Upon my word of honor.
ADAM: Shut up, I say. No single word is true.
LIGHT: Have you this wound since yesterday?
ADAM: No. Today.
  The wound today and yesterday the wig.
  I wore it powdered white upon my head,
  And took it off, I swear it, with my hat,
  Quite by mistake, just as I came indoors.
  What she has washed, that really, I don't know.
  Get the devil out of here, where you belong!
  Into the record-room!   240

  (First Maid exit.)

                    Go. Marguerite!
  Our friend, the sacristan, must lend me his.
  Tell him the cat, the dirty pig, has had
  Her litter in mine this very day. And it
  Now lies befouled beneath my bed. Now I know!
LIGHT: What? The cat? Are you—?
ADAM: As true as I live.
  Five kittens, yellow and black, and one is white.
  The black ones I will drown down in the Vecht.
  What shall I do? Do you want one of them?
LIGHT: And in your wig?
ADAM: May the devil strike me dead!
  My periwig I'd hung quite carefully   250
  Upon a chair, when I was going to bed.
  In the night I touch the chair, the wig falls down—
LIGHT: The cat then takes it in her mouth—
ADAM: My soul—
LIGHT: And drags it under the bed and litters in it.

ADAM: In her mouth? No.—

LIGHT: No? How else?

ADAM: The cat? Oh, what?

LIGHT: No? Or you perhaps?

ADAM: In the mouth? I b'lieve—!
  I kicked it under with my foot this morning.
  When I saw it.

LIGHT: Good, good.

ADAM: What beasts they are!
  They mate and have their young where e're they please.

SECOND MAID (*giggling*): Shall I be going?

ADAM: Yes, and bring my greetings 260
  To Auntie Dressinblack, the sexton's wife.
  Tell her I shall return the wig intact
  This very day—To him you need say nothing.
  You understand me?

SECOND MAID: I'll do just as you say. (*Exit.*)

SCENE 3

Adam and Light.

ADAM: This day, I fear, forebodes us evil, partner.

LIGHT: Pray why?

ADAM: For everything is going topsy-turvy,
  And isn't this a court-day, too?

LIGHT: Of course.
  The plaintiffs are now standing at the door.

ADAM: I dreamt a plaintiff had laid hold of me
  And dragged me here before the seat of justice,   270
  And yet, 'twas I who sat upon the bench
  And scolded, sauced, browbeat my very self,
  And finally put the shackles 'round my neck.

LIGHT: What? You, yourself?

ADAM: Upon my word of honor.
  The two "me's" then became but one and fled,
  And had to spend the night out in the pines.
LIGHT: Well? And the dream, you think—?
ADAM: The devil take it.
  E'en though it's not the dream, some damned old trick,
  Be it what it may, is now at work against me!
LIGHT: A foolish fear! Mete out, as is prescribed,   280
  The while the District Judge is present here,
  Plain justice to all parties 'fore the bar,
  In order that the dream of the judge disgraced
  Be not fulfilled in yet another way.

SCENE 4

The District Judge Walter enters.

The preceding characters.

WALTER: God greet you, Justice Adam.
ADAM: Oh, be welcome!
  Be welcome, gracious Sir, to our fair Huisum!
  Who could, oh gracious Heavens, who ever could,
  Imagine for himself a pleasanter visit.
  I'd ne'er have dreamed that, ere 'twas eight o'clock,
  This morning could have brought me such good fortune.   290
WALTER: I come a little hastily, I know,
  And on this journey in our country's service
  I must be satisfied if all my hosts
  Dismiss me with a friendly "fare-thee-well."
  The meanwhile, I, as far as greetings go,
  In coming bring you greetings from my heart.
  The High Tribunal in Utrecht would improve
  The legal practice in the rural districts,

Which seems to be at fault in many ways.
Malpractice can expect stern reprimand.   300
But my concern upon this trip is not
A stern affair. I'll merely see, not punish.
If I don't find all things as they should be,
I will rejoice if they're but tolerable.
ADAM: In truth such noble thoughts deserve one's praise.
Your Grace will, here and there, I have no doubt,
Find fault with my most antiquated practice.
E'en though it has held sway in Netherlands
Since Emperor Charles the Fifth's most glorious reign.
But what new-fangled ideas people find?   310
The world, a proverb says, grows ever wiser.
I know the whole world's reading Puffendorf,
Yet Huisum's but a small part of the world,
To which not more or less than its small part
Of common wisdom's fund can penetrate.
Bring kindly light to justice here in Huisum
And be assured, O gracious Sir, that you
Will scarce have turned your back on us to leave
Ere justice here will give you satisfaction.
But should you find my office e'en today   320
Good as you wish it, my Soul, it were a wonder,
For I am in the dark to know your will.
WALTER: Quite right! There's need of regulations. Or rather
There are too many. We'll have to sift them out.
ADAM: Yes, through a mighty sieve. Much chaff! Much chaff!
WALTER: Is that your secretary?
LIGHT: Secretary Light,
At your high service, Sir. At Pentecost
Nine years I've filled this high judicial post.
ADAM (*brings a chair.*): Sit down.
WALTER: Don't bother.
ADAM: You come from Holla, then.
WALTER: Just two short miles—But how do you know that?   330
ADAM: How I? Your Grace's servant—
LIGHT: A peasant said so,

Who just arrived here, coming straight from Holla.

WALTER: A peasant?

ADAM: Please your Honor!

WALTER: Yes, a quite
Unpleasant incident befell us there,
Which much perturbed the cheerful mood
Which should accompany us when on such business—
I guess you have been told of it already?

ADAM: Is't true, most gracious Sir, that Justice Paul,
Because he was confined within his house,
The fool, was seized upon by stark despair   340
And hung himself?

WALTER: And made the evil worse.
What first seemed lack of order, mere confusion,
Assumes since then the guise of defalcation,
Which thing, you know, the law cannot excuse.
How many funds have you?

ADAM: Five, if you please.

WALTER: What? Five? 'Twas my belief—Five active funds?
'Twas my belief you had but four—

ADAM: Beg pardon!
With the Funds Collected for the Rhenish Floods?

WALTER: With the Funds Collected for the Overflow!
But now the Rhine is not at overflow,   350
And those collections do not now take place.
But tell me, don't you hold your Court today?

ADAM: If we—

WALTER: What?

LIGHT: Yes, the first day of the week.

WALTER: And that great crowd of people that I saw
Out in your hallway there, are they—?

ADAM: They will—

LIGHT: They are the plaintiffs already thus assembled.

WALTER: This situation suits me fine, my friends.
Just let the people enter, if you please.
I'll witness here your method of procedure
And what the custom is with you in Huisum.   360

The registry and funds we'll check up later,
After the trial itself has been disposed of.
ADAM: Just as you will.—The bailiff! Hey there, Hanfried!

SCENE 5

The Second Servantmaid enters.

The preceding characters.

SECOND MAID: Greetings from the sexton's wife, Judge Adam.
   However much she'd wish the wig—
ADAM: What? No?
SECOND MAID: She says there's preaching in the church this
      morning;
   The sexton himself is wearing one of them.
   His other one she thinks unfit for use.
   And must today be sent to the wigmaker's.
ADAM: Be damned!
SECOND MAID: But once the sexton gets back home,   370
   She'll send his wig to you in haste.
ADAM: Upon my honor, gracious Sir—
WALTER: What is it?
ADAM: A cursed accident has taken both
   My wigs from me. And now the third one, which
   I wished to borrow, cannot be obtained:
   And so I must hold court with head quite bald.
WALTER: Baldheaded!
ADAM: Yes, by the eternal Lord!
   However much, without my wig's assistance,
   I feel concern for my dignity as judge.
   Perhaps I'd try out on my tenant farm,   380
   If by chance my tenant—
WALTER: Out on the farm!
   Can some one else here in the village not—?

ADAM: No, for a fact—

WALTER: The clergyman perhaps.

ADAM: The clergyman? He—

WALTER: Or the schoolmaster.

ADAM: Since tithes in kind, your Honor, have been abolished,
To accomplish which I've given official aid,
I can no longer count on them for favors.

WALTER: Well then, my Village Judge? Well? And the court-
day?
You wish to wait until your hair grows long?

ADAM: If you'll allow, I'll send out to my farm.   390

WALTER: How far is it to the farm?

ADAM: Oh, it is scarcely
Half an hour.

WALTER: Half an hour, what?
The hour for the session has long since struck.
Make haste! I must reach Husahe today.

ADAM: Make haste! Yes—

WALTER: Oh, just powder up your head!
But where the devil did you leave your wig?
Oh, do the best you can, for I must hurry.

ADAM: All right.

THE BAILIFF (enters.): Here is the bailiff.

ADAM: Can I meanwhile
With a good breakfast, sausages from Brunswick,
A little glass of Danziger—

WALTER: No, thanks.   400

ADAM: No trouble!

WALTER: Thanks, I said, I've eaten already.
Go; don't waste your time, and I'll use mine
To make a note upon my memorandum.

ADAM: Well, if you so desire.—Come, Marguerite.

WALTER: You are quite badly bruised, dear Justice Adam.
Have you then fallen?

ADAM: A truly murderous crash
I took this morning as I got out of bed.
You see, Sir District Judge, it was a crash

Into my room, I thought 'twas in my grave.

WALTER: Why that's too bad.—I hope it will not be   410
  Of consequence?

ADAM: I don't think so. And yet,
  In duty's work it shall not hinder me.
  Pardon!

WALTER: Go, go!

ADAM (*to Bailiff*): Go, call the plaintiffs!—March!

(Adam, the Maid and the Bailiff exeunt.)

SCENE 6

Frau Martha, Eve, Veit and Ruprecht enter.

Walter and Light in the background.

FRAU MARTHA: You jug-destroying rabble that you are!
  You'll make amends, you will!

VEIT: Now just be calm,
  Frau Marth'! I'm sure it will all be settled here.

FRAU MARTHA: Oh yes. Be settled. Just see. The clever prattler.
  My jug, the broken one is to be settled.
  Who'll ever settle for my jug that's settled?
  Yes. Here they'll settle that my jug is settled   420
  Once and for all. For such a settlement
  I will not give my upset jug's remains.

VEIT: If you can prove that you are right, you hear me?
  Then I'll replace it.

FRAU MARTHA: You replace my jug.
  If I can prove I'm right, then you'll replace it.
  Just place that jug down there, just try it once.
  Just place it there upon that shelf! Replace it!
  Replace a jug that hasn't a leg to stand on.
  Nor aught to lie, nor aught to sit upon!

VEIT: You heard me! Why your froth? Can one do more?   430
  If one of us has broken your old jug,
  Then you shall get amends.
FRAU MARTHA: I get amends.
  As if a head of my horned cattle were speaking.
  You think the Justice is a potter then?
  E'en if the High and Mighty came and tied
  Their aprons on and put the jug to bake,
  They could more readily make something in
  The jug than mend the damages. Make amends!
RUPRECHT: Come, father, let the dragon be. Hear me.
  It's not the broken jug that's eating her,   440
  But it's the wedding that is broken up,
  And which she hopes to patch with violence here.
  But I, for one, have set my foot upon it:
  And I'll be damned, if e'er I wed that wench.
FRAU MARTHA: The saucy lout! I patch the wedding here!
  The wedding, unbroken, not worth the thread for patching.
  Not worth a single fragment of my jug.
  And if the wedding stood here brightly scoured,
  As yesterday my jug stood on my shelf,
  I'd seize it by the handle with both hands   450
  And, yelling, crash it soundly on his head.
  I have no wish to patch up pieces here.
  To patch it!
EVE: Ruprecht!
RUPRECHT: Out, you!
EVE: Dearest Ruprecht!
RUPRECHT: Out of my sight!
EVE: Oh, I beseech you so!
RUPRECHT: The dissolute—! I dare not mention what.
EVE: Grant me a single word with you in secret—
RUPRECHT: No!
EVE: You soon will join your regiment, oh Ruprecht!
  Who knows, when once your musket you have shouldered,
  If I shall ever see you alive again.
  It's war, remember, war to which you're going.   460

Will you depart from me in such great anger?

RUPRECHT: In anger? No, so help me God, I'll not.

God grant to you prosperity, as much

As he can spare. But if I e'er come back

From out the war with body steeled and sound,

And should I live in Huisum till I'm eighty,

I'd call you till the day I die: a wench!

And you yourself will swear it to the court.

FRAU MARTHA (to Eve): Away! What did you say? Do you
    still wish

To have your self defamed? Our corporal is   470

The man for you, the worthy Woodenlegs,

Who wielded the rod in military service;

And not that idiot there who still must bend

His back to catch the blows. Betrothal and wedding

Are today; and were it also baptism,

I'd be at ease. I'll even suffer my burial

When I've trod that arrogance in the dust

Which swells and topples o'er my jugs.

EVE: Oh Mother!

Oh please forget the jug! Let me go try in town

If some one versed in handicrafts can not   480

Rejoin the fragments so as to suit your pleasure.

And if it can't be mended, take all my savings

And buy yourself a new jug, if you will.

For who would wish for the sake of an earthen jug,

E'en though it dated back to Herod's time,

To raise such racket and to cause such trouble.

FRAU MARTHA: You speak from ignorance. Do you, by chance,

Desire to wear the stocks and in the church,

On Sunday next, stand as a penitent?

Your own good name was lodged within this crock   490

And with it it was ruined before the world;

But not before our God and me and you.

The judge, the executioner is my craftsman.

The block it is and lash of whips we need.

And at the stake that rabble must be burned,

If honor is to burn in pure white flame,
And this jug here's to be reglazed again.

SCENE 7

Adam in his robes of office, but without wig, enters.

The preceding characters.

ADAM (*aside*): Oh Eva. Look! And that square-shouldered rascal,
  That Ruprecht! What the devil! There's his whole tribe!
  They won't accuse and make me my own judge?   500
EVE: Oh dearest mother, come with me, I beg you.
  Let us escape this chamber of misfortune!
ADAM: Old fellow! Tell me: what's the case they bring?
LIGHT: What do I know? It's noise for naught, mere trifles.
  I hear that some one has broken up a jug.
ADAM: A jug! So, so!—Oh, who then broke the jug?
LIGHT: Who has broken it?
ADAM: Yes, dear old fellow.
LIGHT: My Soul! Sit down; then you will soon find out.
ADAM (*secretly*): Dear Eve!
EVE (*likewise*):   Go 'way!
ADAM: One word.
EVE: I will hear nothing.
ADAM: Why are you here?
EVE: I tell you to go 'way.   510
ADAM: Eve dear! I beg you! What does all this mean?
EVE: If you don't straight—! I say; let me alone.
ADAM (*to Light*): Old fellow, listen, my Soul! I cannot stand it.
  The wound here on my shin-bone turns my stomach.
  You hear the case and I will go to bed.
LIGHT: To bed—? You wish—? I b'lieve that you are crazy.
ADAM: The devil take it. I fear that I must vomit.
LIGHT: I b'lieve you're really crazy. You've just now come—?
  For all I care. Then tell the District Judge.

He might allow it.—I don't know what ails you.   520
ADAM (*again to Eve*): My Eva, dear, I beg you! By all the
   wounds!
   What is it you bring me here?
EVE: You'll soon find out.
ADAM: Is it just the jug there, which your mother's holding,
   Which I, as far—?
EVE: Yes, just the broken jug.
ADAM: And nothing else?
EVE: Naught else.
ADAM: No? Nothing else?
EVE: I tell you go, and let me be in peace.
ADAM: Hear me, by Heavens, be wise! That's my advice.
EVE: You shameless thing!
ADAM: Here in the note now stands
   The name in giant letters, Ruprecht Dimpel.
   I carry it ripe and ready in my pocket.   530
   You hear it crackle, Eva? See, you can,
   Upon my honor, fetch it in a year
   To cut out mourning bodices and aprons.
   When you have heard that Ruprecht in Batavia
   Cashed in—I know not of what sort of illness,
   Of yellow, scarlet or of putrid fever.
WALTER: Don't speak with the contestants, Justice Adam,
   Before the session! Sit down and question them.
ADAM: What did he say? What does Your Grace command?
WALTER: What I command? I thought I told you plainly,   540
   That you should not in secret before the session
   Indulge in doubtful talk with litigants.
   Here is the place which most befits your office,
   A public trial is what I'm waiting for.
ADAM (*aside*): Be damned! I can't make up my mind about it—!
   —And something crashed just as I took my leave—
LIGHT (*arousing him*): Your Honor! Are you—?
ADAM: I? No. Upon my honor!
   I hung my wig upon it carefully
   And must have been an ox—

LIGHT: What?

ADAM: What?

LIGHT: I asked—!

ADAM: You asked if I—?

LIGHT: If you are deaf, I asked. 550
His Grace himself has just called to you.

ADAM: I thought—! Who calls?

LIGHT: The District Justice there.

ADAM (*to himself*): Oh! The devil take it all! There are
two ways,
By Heaven; no more. What doesn't bend must break.
At once! At once! What does Your Grace command?
Shall I begin the trial at once?

WALTER: You are peculiarly distraught. What's wrong?

ADAM: My word! Beg pardon. One of my guinea hens,
That I just purchased from an Indian sailor,
Has pip. I ought to cram it, but I don't know how; 560
And so I asked that maiden for advice.
I am a fool about such things, you see.
My chickens are the things I call my children.

WALTER: Sit down here. Call the plaintiff and examine him.
And you, our Clerk, you will record the minutes.

ADAM: Does your Grace wish to have this trial conducted
According to formalities of the law.
Or as the custom is right here in Huisum?

WALTER: According to the formalities of the law,
As it is practiced in Huisum, not otherwise. 570

ADAM: Fine! Fine! I'll strive to do it as you wish.
You're ready then, my Clerk?

LIGHT: Yes, at your service.

ADAM: Then Justice take your unretarded course!
Plaintiff now step up!

FRAU MARTHA: Here, Village Judge!

ADAM: Who are you?

FRAU MARTHA: Who—?

ADAM: You.

FRAU MARTHA: Who—I—?

ADAM: Who are you?
  What name, what rank, the place you live, and so on.
FRAU MARTHA: I b'lieve you're joking, Judge.
ADAM: I, joking? What?
  I sit here in the name of Justice, Frau Martha,
  And Justice now must know just who you are.
LIGHT (*half aloud*): Say, drop such useless questioning—   580
FRAU MARTHA: You look
  In, Sundays, through my window, when you go
  To see your country-place!
WALTER: You know the woman?
ADAM: She lives just 'round the corner here, Your Grace,
  Just where the footpath crosses through the hedge;
  Widow of a lodge-keeper, a midwife now,
  An honest woman and beyond reproach.
WALTER: If you are then so well-informed, Your Honor,
  All questions of this nature are superfluous.
  Write down her name into the record-book
  And put beside it: "Well-known to the Court."   590
ADAM: That too. You are not for formalities.
  Then do just as His Grace would have it done.
WALTER: Now ask about the nature of her plea.
ADAM: Now shall I—?
WALTER: Yes, find out her purpose here!
ADAM: It is, I'm sure, a jug.
WALTER: What's that? You're sure!
ADAM: A jug. A simple jug. Write down: "A jug,"
  And put beside it: "Well-known to the Court."
LIGHT: Upon the speculation which I chanced
  Will you, your Honor—?
ADAM: By Heavens, if I say it,
  Then write it down. Is it not a jug, Frau Martha?   600
FRAU MARTHA: Yes, this jug here—
ADAM: You see!
FRAU MARTHA: This broken one—
ADAM: A case of pedantry and scruples.
LIGHT: I beg you.

ADAM: And who, then, broke the jug? Of course, that rascal—?
FRAU MARTHA: Yes, he, that rascal there—.
ADAM (aside): I need no more.
RUPRECHT: That is not true, your Honor.
ADAM (aside): Up, up, revive, you old man Adam!
RUPRECHT: She's lying to your very face—
ADAM: Shut up, young fool!
    You'll put your neck in fetters soon enough.
    Write down "a jug" then, Clerk, just as I said,
    Together with the name of him who smashed it.
    The facts will now be straightway ascertained.
WALTER: Your Honor! What a violent way of acting.
ADAM: How so?
LIGHT: Will you not form'lly—?
ADAM: No! I say;
    Your Grace cares naught for bare formalities.
WALTER: If you, Sir Justice Adam, do not know
    The method of procedure in this case,
    Here's not the time and place to teach it to you.
    If you can't mete out justice better than this,
    Then yield your seat, perhaps your clerk here can.
ADAM: Beg pardon. I did as here in Huisum is the custom.
    Your Grace moreover ordered me to do so.   620
WALTER: What? I?
ADAM: Upon my honor!
WALTER: I ordered you
    To render justice according to the laws.
    The laws in Huisum, it was my belief,
    Were those which govern everywhere in Holland.
ADAM: I must implore your Grace's most humble pardon!
    We have in Huisum, with your kind permission,
    Some statutes to ourselves alone peculiar,
    Not written, to be sure, but none the less
    Inherited by us through tried tradition,
    And from this code, I'm bold enough to hope,   630
    I have this day not strayed e'en one iota.
    But I'm familiar with your other code,

As it is practiced elsewhere in the kingdom.
Would you have proof! All right, just give me orders!
I can deal justice in one way or the other.
WALTER: I fear you put false meaning on my words.
So be it. Start the trial anew again.—
ADAM: My word! Give heed and you'll be satisfied.
Frau Martha Rull! Will you present your plaint?
FRAU MARTHA: My plaint, you know, concerns this jug of
   mine.   640
But grant that I, before I here explain
What has befallen my jug, also describe
What it has meant to me.
ADAM: This is your chance.
FRAU MARTHA: You see this jug, most worthy, reverend Sirs?
You see this jug?
ADAM: Oh yes, of course we see it.
FRAU MARTHA: No, pardon me, you see naught but the fragments.
The most beautiful of jugs is rudely shattered.
Right here, where now's a hole, where you see naught,
The United Provinces of the Netherlands
Were handed over to the Spaniard Philip.   650
Here, in imperial robes stood Charles the Fifth:
Of whom you see his legs alone left standing.
Here Philip knelt as he received the crown:
He now lies in the pot up to the rear
Which also has received a blow, alas.
There his two cousins fair, the queens of France
And Hungary, wiped, the both quite moved, the tears
From out their eyes. When now you see the one
Raise up her hand which holds a handkerchief,
It is as though she wept but for herself.   660
Here in the train stands bold Sir Philibert
(Protecting whom the emperor caught the blow.)
And still leans on his sword. But he should fall,
As well as Maximilian, the rogue!
For under them their swords are broken away.
Here in the middle, in his sacred mitre,

The Archbishop of Arras formerly stood.
But him the devil has taken hide and hair.
His lengthy shadow alone falls o'er the pavement.
Here in the background stood the body-guard   670
With hallebards and spears in close array;
Here houses on the market-place in Brussels.
Here peeps a prying soul from out his window.
But what he now can see I do not know.

ADAM: Frau Marth'! Spare us the treaty long since scrapped,
Unless it it has some bearing on the case.
The hole alone, and not the provinces
Whose transfer was described, is our concern.

FRAU MARTHA: The beauty of the jug does have some bearing!
The jug was taken as booty by Childeric,   680
The boilermender, when the Prince of Orange
Took Briel with his bold band of mendicants.
Filled with wine, a Spaniard lifted it
Just to his eager mouth when Childeric
Cut down the Spaniard, hitting from behind,
And seized the jug and drained it and went on.

ADAM: A worthy mendicant.

FRAU MARTHA: Inheritance
Then gave the jug to Feargod, who dug graves.
He drank from it but thrice, the sober chap,
And each time were its contents mixed with water.   690
The first time when, already sixty years,
He married a young wife. Then, three years later,
When he by her became a happy father,
And, after she had borne him sixteen children,
He drank from it the third time, when she died.

ADAM: Fine! That's not bad at all.

FRAU MARTHA: The jug then came
To Zacchaeus, the tailor out in Tirlemont,
Who told with his own mouth to my dead husband,
That which I now desire to tell to you.
When some French troops were plundering, he threw   700
His jug and household goods out through the window.

He too sprang out and broke his neck, the clown.
This earthen jug, this fragile jug of clay,
However, fell and yet it stood unbroken.
ADAM: Come to the point! I beg you, Martha Rull.
FRAU MARTHA: In the great fire back in sixty-six
My husband had it then, God bless his soul—
ADAM: The devil! Woman! Are you not yet finished?
FRAU MARTHA: If you won't let me speak, Sir Justice Adam,
Then I've come here in vain, and now I'll go   710
And seek a court where I'll at least be heard.
WALTER: You shall speak here; but not of matters which
Are foreign to your plea. If you but tell us
Your jug was treasured much, then we shall know
As much as we as judges need to know.
FRAU MARTHA: How much you need to know to judge this case
I do not know and do not seek to know.
But this I know that I, to press my case,
Must be allowed to speak at least of something.
WALTER: All right. To close now, what befell the jug?   720
What? What befell the jug in that great fire
In anno sixty-six? Will you not tell us?
What did befall the jug?
FRAU MARTHA: What then befell it?
Nothing, Sirs, I do declare that nothing
Befell the jug in anno six and sixty.
The jug remained quite whole among the flames
And from the ashes of the house I pulled it,
Both glazed and shining on the morning after,
As if it came straight from the potter's oven.
WALTER: That's good. And now we know the jug. We know 730
What has befallen it and what has not.
What is there more?
FRAU MARTHA: Now this jug here, you see—this jug,
A jug, though broken, worthy yet to be
The jug to grace a noble lady's mouth,
And not unworthy of the regent's lips,
This jug, you two most high and worthy judges,

This jug of mine that rascal there has broken.
ADAM: Who?
FRAU MARTHA: He, that Ruprecht there.
RUPRECHT: That is a lie,
Your Honor.
ADAM: Hold your tongue until you're asked.
You'll have a chance to speak sometime today.   740
Have you recorded that in the minutes?
LIGHT: Oh yes.
ADAM: Relate what happened, worthy Mistress Martha.
FRAU MARTHA: 'Twas yesterday at 'leven—
ADAM: When, did you say?
FRAU MARTHA: At 'leven.
ADAM: In the morning?
FRAU MARTHA: No, pardon me, at night—
I lie in bed and wish to dim the lamp,
When loud male voices like a very tumult,
Out of my daughter's chamber, far from mine,
As if old Nick'd broken in, quite frighten me.
I hasten quickly down the stairs and find
Her chamber door is broken in by force;   750
And angry, scolding voices strike my ear.
And when I then make a light upon the scene,
What do I find, Sir Judge? What do I find?
I find the jug lying shattered in the chamber;
In every corner lies a piece.
My daughter wrings her hands, and that jay there,
He fumes like mad in the middle of the room.
ADAM: Oh, curses!
FRAU MARTHA: What!
ADAM: See here, Frau Martha!
FRAU MARTHA: Yes!
And then, as if in my all-righteous rage
Ten arms were added unto me, I feel   760
As though each one were armed with vulture's talons.
I then begin to question him: What he,
So late at night, desires and why in rage

He broke the jugs he found here in my house.
And can you guess the answer that he gives?
The shameless fellow! Scoundrel that he is!
I'll see him on the rack, or ne'er again
Will rest my weary back upon a bed.
He says another man has knocked the jug
From off the shelf—, another, think of it,   770
Who just has fled from him out of the chamber;
And heaps abuse upon my girl and me.

ADAM: A mere red herring. And then?

FRAU MARTHA: When he speaks thus
I look inquiring at my girl who stands
There like a corpse. I say to her: "My Eve!"—
She seats herself. "Was it some other man?"
I ask. And she cries out: "By Joseph and the Virgin!
What do you think then, Mother?" "Then speak! Who was it?"
"Who else?"—says she. And who else could it be?
And then she swears to me that he had done it.   780

EVE: What did I swear? What did I swear to you?
I swore you nothing. No—!

FRAU MARTHA: Eve!

EVE: No. You're lying—.

RUPRECHT: There you hear it.

ADAM: Shut up, you cursed hound!
If you don't want my fist to stop your throat!
Your turn comes afterwards, not now.

FRAU MARTHA: You say you didn't—?

EVE: No, mother, you're deceiving.
It pains me to the bottom of my soul
That I must publicly declare this here:
But I've sworn nothing, nothing have I sworn.

ADAM: But act with sense then, children.

LIGHT: That's quite strange.   790

FRAU MARTHA: But didn't you assure me, oh my Eva—?
Did you not call on Joseph and the Virgin?

EVE: Not as an oath! Not swearing! See, this I swear to,
And call upon Saint Joseph and the Virgin.

ADAM: Oh friends! Oh now, Frau Martha! What are you doing?
How you intimidate that poor, good child!
When she has had a chance to think it over,
And calmly has recalled all that has happened,
—I say all that has happened and that which still
Can happen, should she not speak quite as she ought,—   800
Just watch, she'll tell us all today as yesterday,
No matter whether she swears to it or not.
Let Joseph and the Virgin out of this game.
WALTER: Oh no, your Honor, no! Whoever could wish
To teach the litigants such doubtful tactics?
FRAU MARTHA: If she can tell me to my very face,
The shameless, dissolute hussy that she is,
That it was some one else, and not that Ruprecht,
Then she, for all of me, can—, I won't say what.
But I, your Honor, I assure you this,   810
Although I can't affirm she swore to it:
That she did say it yesterday, that I'll swear,
And Joseph and the Virgin I call to witness.
ADAM: And now the girl no longer will—
WALTER: Your Honor!
ADAM: Your Grace?—What is't?—Isn't it so, dear Eve?
FRAU MARTHA: Now out with it! Did you not tell me that?
Didn't you tell me yesterday? Didn't you?
EVE: Who denies I said it—.
ADAM: There you have it.
RUPRECHT: The dirty wench!
ADAM: Make note.
VEIT: Fie, shame on her.
WALTER: Of this performance of yours, Sir Justice Adam,   820
I know not what to think. If you yourself
Had broken the jug in question, you could not
Attempt more energetically to shift suspicion
From your own person to this young man here.
Hear, Clerk; I'll hope you'll enter into your records
Naught save the fact the maiden now admits
Her yesterday's confession, but not the deed.

—Is it now the maiden's turn to make a statement?

ADAM: My soul, if it is not her turn just yet,
  In such things human nature errs, Your Grace.   830
  Whom should I now interrogate? The accused?
  My word! I always take advice that's good.

WALTER: How very naïve! Yes, question the accused.
  Question and make an end of it. Please do!
  This is the last case you will ever try.

ADAM: The last one! What! Yes, really! The accused!
  What were you thinking of this time, old judge?
  Cursed be my guinea hen that has the pip!
  Had it but croaked of the plague in India!
  That noodle-dumpling is always on my mind.   840

WALTER: What's on? What sort of dumpling is on—

ADAM: The noodle-dumpling
  Which, with your pardon, I wished to give my hen.
  And if the beast won't swallow down the pill,
  My soul, I do not know just what will happen.

WALTER: Just do your duty, I tell you, by perdition!

ADAM: Defendant, now come forth.

RUPRECHT: I'm here, your Honor.
  Ruprecht, Veit's, the cotter's son, of Huisum.

ADAM: Have you then heard what in this court just now
  Frau Martha dared to testify against you?

RUPRECHT: Yes, Sir Village Judge, I heard it.

ADAM: Will you then dare   850
  To offer opposition to it? Huh?
  Do you confess or dare you undertake
  To disavow it, a God-forgotten man?

RUPRECHT: What have I to oppose to her accusal,
  Your Honor? Oh, with your kind permission,
  No word that she has spoken here is true.

ADAM: So? And that you think that you can prove?

RUPRECHT: Oh yes.

ADAM: The honorable Frau Martha there—
  Let her keep cool and calm. We'll soon find out.

WALTER: Why should Frau Martha cause the Judge concern?   860

ADAM: Why me—? By God! Should I, a Christian—?
WALTER: Report
  What you would adduce in your behalf.
  Do you know, Clerk, how to conduct a trial?
ADAM: What? What?
LIGHT: If I—oh, well, well, if your Highness—
ADAM: Why do you stare? What have you to depose?
  Does not the ass stand there just like an ox?
  What have you to depose?
RUPRECHT: What I depose?
WALTER: Yes, you. It's you must now relate the story.
RUPRECHT: My soul, if they would only let me speak.
WALTER: Why, Judge! Such conduct cannot be endured.   870
RUPRECHT: It mighta been 'bout ten o'clock at night,—
  A January night, but just as warm
  As May. Then I say to my father: "Father!
  I want to go and visit Eve a little."
  For you must know I was to marry her.
  A sturdy gal she is. I noticed how
  At harvest time she handled work with ease.
  The hay flew fast, just like a frightened mouse.
  I asked her: "Will you?" and she answered: "Oh!
  How you do cackle." Then later she said: "Yes."   880
ADAM: Let him stick to his subject. Cackle! What?
  I asked her "Will you?" And she answered "Yes."
RUPRECHT: Yes, on my word, your Honor.
WALTER: Further! Further!
RUPRECHT: Well—
  Then I said: "Father, listen! Will you let me?"
  A little while we chatted by the window.
  "Well," says he, "run along. You'll stay outdoors?"
  "Yes, by my Soul," say I, "I'll swear to that."
  "Well, go,' says he, "but be back here by 'leven."
ADAM: Go on and talk and cackle without end,
  Well, will you soon quit talking?
RUPRECHT: "Well," say I: 890
  "That is agreed." And I put on my cap

And go; and try to take the bridge and
Go back through town, because the brook was swollen.
Hell and damnation, Ruprecht! then I thought.
Now Martha's garden-gate is surely closed.
For just till ten the daughter leaves it open.
If I'm not there by ten I do not come.
ADAM: Such low-down way of doing things.
WALTER: And then?
RUPRECHT: Then—as I pass beneath the linden-lane,
    Near Martha's, where the trees are thickly arched,   900
    And darker than the minster is in Utrecht,
    I hear the distant garden-gate a-creaking.
    See there! There is my Eva still! I say
    And send my eyes with joy to that dark spot
    From whence my ears had brought me the report—
    And call them blind, when they return to me,
    And send them quickly forth the second time,
    That they might search the better. Then I scold
    Them, good-for-nothing slanderers, and worse,
    Inciters, low-down scandal-mongers,   910
    And send them forth a third time and I think
    That, having done their duty, they madly want
    To leap from out my head and give themselves
    Into some other service than my own.
    It is my Eve. I know her by her dress.
    Another man is with her, too.
ADAM: So? Still another? Who? You babbling fool!
RUPRECHT: Who? Yes, my Soul! Do you ask me? Well?
ADAM: Oh well!
    Whom you did not take we cannot wake, I guess.
WALTER: On! Further with your speech! Let him alone!   920
    Why do you interrupt him, Village Judge?
RUPRECHT: I cannot swear it by the Sacrament.
    Pitch-dark it was, and then all cats are gray.
    But you must know that he who mends our shoes,
    That Lebrecht, who was late a 'prentice-boy,
    Has long been running 'round to see my gal.

I told her 'way last Autumn: "Eve, look here;
That rogue hangs 'round your house and I don't like it.
Tell him that you're no pickings for his kind,
Or, by my soul, I'll throw him out of doors."   930
She says: "You're vexing," and she tells him something
That's neither here nor there, nor fish nor fowl.
Then I go in and throw the rascal out.

ADAM: The rascal's name is Lebrecht?

RUPRECHT: Yes, Lebrecht.

ADAM: Good.
We have a name. The rest we'll soon find out.
Have you recorded that in the minutes, Clerk?

LIGHT: Oh, yes, and all the rest, so please Your Honor.

ADAM: Speak on, then, Ruprecht, my dear son.

RUPRECHT: And now,
When after eleven I meet this loving pair,
—I always left at ten—my eyes are opened.   940
I think: Wait, Ruprecht, still you have a chance.
The stag's horns do not yet adorn your brow.
You must take care and feel your brow once more
To see if horns have started sprouting there.
I gently enter through the garden-gate
And hide myself behind the old yew-hedge.
I hear a whispering here, a joking there,
A tugging and a scuffling too, your Honor.
My Soul! I think. I shall for longing—

EVE: You villain!
Oh, how disgraceful 'tis of you!

FRAU MARTHA: You scoundrel!   950
I'll show you yet, when I get you alone,
That I have teeth, just wait! You don't yet know
The stuff I am made of! But you'll soon find out!

RUPRECHT: A quarter-hour they act thus. Then I think
Whate'er comes next, today is sure no wedding?
And ere I was quite finished with this thought,
Whiz!! they're in the house before seeing the parson.

EVE: Go, Mother, now let happen whatever will—

ADAM: Shut up, you there, I say. The thunder storm
    Strikes down on you, you uninvited gossip!   960
    Wait till I call on you to make your speech.

WALTER: Quite strange indeed, by Heavens!

RUPRECHT: My blood, Judge Adam, now boils
    As if an artery would break. Air! Air!
    A button springs off my doublet. Air, now!
    I pull my doublet off and cry: "Air! Air!"
    And go and push and kick and thunder there,
    On finding that the hussy's door is locked,
    Till with one mighty kick I push it in.

ADAM: Bright boy you are!

RUPRECHT: Just as it rattles open,
    The jug falls down off the shelf inside,   970
    And—whiz!—a man jumps out the window too.
    I just can see his coat-tails flying after.

ADAM: Was it that Lebrecht?

RUPRECHT: Who else then, your Honor?
    The girl stands there. I push her in a heap,
    And hastening to the window, find the scamp
    Still hanging on the pickets of the trellis,
    There, where the grape-vine twines up to the roof.
    And since the door-knob clung tight in my hand
    When I came thundering in, I slam him one
    With that great pound of steel straight on his pate   980
    Which, by good chance, your Honor, I just could reach.

ADAM: Was it a knob?

RUPRECHT: What?

ADAM: Was it—?

RUPRECHT: Yes, a door-knob, yes.

ADAM: That's why.—

LIGHT: You thought, perhaps, it was a dagger?

ADAM: A dagger? I—? How's that?

RUPRECHT: A dagger.

LIGHT: Oh, well!
    One can sometimes hear wrong. A door-knob, too,
    Has very much in common with a dagger.

ADAM: I think—!

LIGHT: Upon my word! The shaft, your Honor?

ADAM: The shaft!

RUPRECHT: The shaft! But that's not what it was.
It was the other end of that old knob.

ADAM: The other end of that old knob it was!   990

LIGHT: So! So!

RUPRECHT: But on the handle was a lump of
Lead like a dagger's hilt; that I must say.

ADAM: Yes, like a hilt.

LIGHT: Good. Like a dagger's hilt.
A weapon of some dreadful sort it surely
Must have been. That I knew well.

WALTER: To business, Sirs. Now please keep to your business!

ADAM: Naught but tomfoolery, Sir Clerk! Proceed!

RUPRECHT: The scamp falls down and I'm about to turn
When in the dark I see him getting up.
I think: "You still alive?," climb to the window   1000
And wish to put an end to all his going.
When now, my Sirs, as I'm about to jump
A mighty handful of sharp, coarse-grained sand
Scattering like hail flies straight into my eyes.
—And man and night and world and window sill
On which I stand, it seems, so help me God,
All fall together in one heap of darkness.

ADAM: Be damned! See that! Who did it?

RUPRECHT: Who? That Lebrecht.

ADAM: That scoundrel!

RUPRECHT: My word! If it was really he.

ADAM: Who else?

RUPRECHT: As if a rain-storm pitched me down   1010
Ten fathoms from a mountain to an abyss,
Thus do I fall from off the window sill.
It seems as though I'm crashing through the floor.
And still I do not break my neck, nor yet
My back, nor hip, nor aught; but in this time
I lost my chance to lay hands on that scamp.

Then I sit up and wipe my injured eyes.
She comes and cries: "O Lord! O my poor Ruprecht!"
"What's injured you?" My Soul! I raised my foot,
'Twas good I did not see which way I kicked.—   1020
ADAM: And did the sand cause that?
RUPRECHT: That blast of sand.
ADAM: By God! Well aimed!
RUPRECHT: And then, when I get up,
Why should I soil my fists upon her here?
I scold her and I call her: low-down wench,
And think that such is good enough for her,
But tears well up to choke my very words,
For when Frau Martha comes into the room
And brings a lamp and I behold the girl
Who stands before me trembling, that's a pity,
She who was wont to look so free from care,   1030
Then to myself I say: The blind are blessed.
And I'd have given my eyes to whom so willed
That he might play a game of marbles with them.
EVE: He doesn't deserve, the villain—
ADAM: Will you keep quiet!
RUPRECHT: The rest you know.
ADAM: What do you mean—the rest?
RUPRECHT: Oh well, Frau Martha came and spilled her venom,
And Ralph, their neighbor, came and neighbor Hinz,
And cousin Sue and cousin Liza came,
And men and maids, and dogs and cats all came.
It was a spectacle. Frau Martha asked   1040
The maiden there: Who it was that smashed the jug;
And she, she said, you know, that I had done it.
My Soul, she wasn't very wrong, dear Sirs,
I smashed the mug which she used once too often,
And now a hole adorns the cobbler's head.—
ADAM: Frau Martha! What reply would you now make?
Speak up?
FRAU MARTHA: What I'd reply to such as that?
His speech, your Honor, comes stealing like a martin

And strangles truth as 'twere a cackling hen.
Whoe'er loves justice should seize a mighty club   1050
And quite wipe out this monster of the night.
ADAM: Then you will have to furnish us the proof.
FRAU MARTHA: Oh yes, indeed. Here is my witness. Speak.
ADAM: Your daughter? No, Frau Martha.
WALTER: No? Why not?
ADAM: As witness, gracious Sir? Does not the law-book say,
    In section *quarto* is it? Or in *quinto*?
    When jugs, or what they be—how should I know?—
    Are smashed or broken by young jackanapes,
    Then daughters may not witness for their mothers?
WALTER: Within your head lie knowledge and base error   1060
    Completely kneaded together like a dough.
    With every piece you give me some of each.
    The girl's not yet a witness, she but explains now.
    If, and for whom, she can and will bear witness
    Will first be learned from this, her explanation.
ADAM: Yes, explanation. Good. In section *sexto*.
    But what she says one won't believe.
WALTER: Step up, my dear young child.
ADAM: Hey, Liz'!—Beg pardon!
    My tongue's become quite parched.—Oh, Marguerite!

SCENE 8

A Maid enters.

The preceding characters.

ADAM: A glass of water!—
THE MAID: ·   At once.
ADAM: Will you not also—?   1070
WALTER: No, thank you.
ADAM: French or Moselle? Whate'er you wish.

    (*Walter bows; The Maid brings water and departs.*)

SCENE 9

Walter, Adam, Frau Martha, etc., without the maid.

ADAM: If I may freely speak my will, your Grace,
This case seems fitted for a compromise.
WALTER: For compromise? That is not clear, Your Honor.
Intell'gent folk can surely compromise,
But how you would effect such thing already,
Now, when the case has not been unravelled,
It would indeed give me great joy to hear.
How do you think you'd bring that end about?
Have you so soon a fixed opinion?
ADAM: My soul!   1080
If I, since law doth leave me in the lurch,
Should call philosophy to be my aid,
Then 'twas—that Lebrecht.
WALTER: Who?
ADAM: Or Ruprecht there.
WALTER: Who?
ADAM: Or Lebrecht—who smashed up the jug.
WALTER: Who was it then? Was't Lebrecht or was't Ruprecht?
You're groping with your judgment, so it seems,
Just like a hand in a full bag of peas.
ADAM: Permit!
WALTER: Be quiet, please.
ADAM: Well, as you will.
Upon my word 'twould be all right with me
If it were both of them that did the deed.   1090
WALTER: Ask there and you'll find out.
ADAM: Most gladly, Sir.
But I'll be damned if you will find it out.
Have you your minute-book now all prepared?
LIGHT: Completely.
ADAM: Good.
LIGHT: I start a brand new page

And yearn to know what will be written on it.
ADAM: A brand new page? That's fine.
WALTER: Speak now, my child.
ADAM: Speak, Eva, don't you hear? Speak now, Miss Eva!
Give God, you hear, my dear, give, oh my soul,
Him and the world, give him aught of the truth.
Think that you stand there 'fore God's judgment seat   1100
And you must never dare aggrieve your judge
With falsehood and with chatter which does not
Concern this case. Oh yes! You're sensible.
A judge, you know, is ever but a justice,
Today he serves this one, tomorrow that.
If you should say 'twas Lebrecht, all is well!
And should you say 'twas Ruprecht, also well!
Speak thus, or thus, and I'm no honest man
If things don't happen just as you would have them.
If you should wish to gossip of another,   1110
A third, perchance, and mention stupid names,
Then, child, take care; I'll tell you nothing further.
In Huisum, damn it, no one will believe you,
And no one, Eva, in the Netherlands.
You know the white-washed walls can tell no tales.
He, too, will know how to defend himself,
And great misfortune will befall your Ruprecht.
WALTER: If you would only let your talking be!
It's idle gossip without point or plan.
ADAM: Do you not understand it, Sir?
WALTER: Get on!   1120
Too long you've spoken idly from the bench.
ADAM: Surely, Sir, I am no learned man.
And if I'm not quite clear to men from Utrecht,
Perhaps it's different with the plain folk here.
I'll bet the maiden knows just what I wish.
FRAU MARTHA: What is all this? Speak boldly what you know!
EVE: Oh dearest mother!
FRAU MARTHA: You! I'm warning you!
RUPRECHT: My Soul! Frau Martha, it's hard to speak out bold

RUPRECHT: No, Auntie is at home.   1440
WALTER: At home. 'Tis well.
RUPRECHT: She'll be be here right away.
WALTER: She'll be here right away. Bring forth the wine.
ADAM (*aside*): Be damned!
WALTER: Make haste. But nothing will I eat
  Except a piece of dry bread and some salt.
ADAM (*aside*): For but two moments with the gal alone—
  (*aloud*): What! But dry bread! And salt! Go on.
WALTER: Oh yes.
ADAM: At least a piece of good Limburger checse—
  Cheese whets the tongue that it may taste the wine.
WALTER: All right. A piece of cheese, but nothing else.
ADAM: Now go and spread the cloth of damask white.   1450
  Let all be plain but good.

  (*Maid exit.*)

    That's the advantage
  With us damned bachelor-folk. What others are
  Compelled each day to share with care and sparing
  With wife and children, we, whene'er we please
  With some good friend, completely unconcerned,
  Enjoy in full.
WALTER: But what I wished to say—
  Where did you get that wound of yours, dear Judge?
  A wicked hole, forsooth, that in your head!
ADAM: — I fell.
WALTER: You fell. Oh, so. When? Was't last evening?
ADAM: Today at half past five. This morning, Sir.   1460
  Just as I wished to rise from out my bed.
WALTER: Over what?
ADAM: Over—Gracious District Judge.
  To tell the truth, I stumbled o'er myself.
  I fell head foremost up against my stove,
  Until this hour I really don't know why.
WALTER: Fell backwards?
ADAM: What? Fall backwards?

WALTER: Or face first?
You have two wounds, one forward and one aft.
ADAM: Both front and back. Oh Marguerite!

(*Both maids enter with wine, etc. They set the table and
exeunt.*)

WALTER: What's that?
ADAM: First thus, then thus. First on the stove's sharp edge,
Which pushed my brow in here, and then I fell   1470
Down backwards to the floor and there I struck
The back part of my head a fearful blow.

(*Pours out wine.*)

Will you drink, Sir?
WALTER (*takes the glass*): If you but had a wife,
I should imagine the case quite differently,
Sir, Justice.
ADAM: How so?
WALTER: Yes, 'pon my honor,
I see you scraped and scratched all over so.
ADAM (*laughs*): No, God be thanked! It's not from woman's nails.
WALTER: Another advantage for the bachelors, I believe.
ADAM (*continuing to laugh*): Branches for my silk-worms that
were placed
There in the corner by the stove to dry.   1480
And now, here's to your health!

(*They drink.*)

WALTER: And just today
To lose your periwig in such strange manner!
It would at least have hidden your wounds for you.
ADAM: Yes, yes, but evils always come as twins.
Here.—This is nice and fat.—May I?—
WALTER: A bit.
Is't Limberg?
ADAM: D'rect from Limberg, worthy Sir.
WALTER: And how the devil did you say that happened?
ADAM: What?

WALTER: That you have parted with your periwig.

ADAM: You see, last evening I sat down to read
  A document, and since I had mislaid   1490
  My glasses, I bent down so low to read
  The case, that by the candle-flame's bright glow
  My periwig caught fire. I, I think:
  Fire falls from Heaven upon my sinful head,
  And seize the wig to cast it far from me;
  But ere I have unloosed the ribbon-ties
  The wig flames up like Sodom and Gomorrah
  So that I barely save my last three hairs.

WALTER: Hm, curses! And your other one's in town?

ADAM: Yes, at the periwig-maker's.—But let's to business. 1500

WALTER: But not too fast, I beg you, Justice Adam.

ADAM: Oh, well! The hours fly. Here, have a glass.

  (*He pours out wine.*)

WALTER: Poor Lebrecht—if that codger told the truth—
  Has likewise had a very wicked fall.

ADAM: Upon my honor. (*He drinks.*)

WALTER: And if the case before us
  Remains unraveled,—I almost fear it will—
  You will be able, here in your small town
  To recognize the culprit by his wounds. (*He drinks.*)
  Niersteiner wine?

ADAM: What?

WALTER: Or good Oppenheimer?

ADAM: Niersteiner. Look! 'pon my honor! You can tell.   1510
  From Nierstein, gracious Sir, as if I'd fetched it.

WALTER: I tried it at the wine press three years ago.

  (*Adam pours out wine again.*)

  How high then is your window?—You! Frau Martha!

FRAU MARTHA: My window?

WALTER: The window of that chamber, yes,
  In which the maiden sleeps?

FRAU MARTHA: Her chamber is

But in the second floor, a cellar beneath it,
The window scarcely nine feet from the ground.
And yet the whole quite well-thought-out arrangement
Is very awkward if one wants to jump.
For two feet from the wall a grape vine stands   1520
Which spreads its knotty branches on the trellis,
That runs along the wall's entire length.
The very window is entwined in vines.
A boar well-armed with heavy tusks would have
A heavy task to break his way through this.
ADAM: And none hung in it either.

(*He fills his glass.*)

WALTER: What's that?
ADAM: Nothing! (*He drinks.*)
WALTER (*to Ruprecht*): Where did you hit the sinner? On the
    head?
ADAM: Here.
WALTER: Wait.
ADAM: Giv't here.
WALTER: It's still half full.
ADAM: I'll fill it.
WALTER: You hear?
ADAM: Oh, just to make good measure.
WALTER: I beg you.
ADAM: According to the Pythagorean rule.   1530

(*He fills his glass.*)

WALTER (*again to Ruprecht*): How often did you hit the sinner's
    head?
ADAM: One is the Lord; the second, Chaos black;
    The third, the World. Three glasses have my praise.
    Of the third glass each drop tastes like a Sun,
    And each succeeding glass like firmaments.
WALTER: How often did you hit the sinner's head?
    You Ruprecht, you I ask!
ADAM: Now shall we hear it?

How often did you hit the 'scape-goat? Speak!
Lord's sake, the fellow doesn't know if he—
Have you forgot?
RUPRECHT: With the door-knob?
ADAM: Yes, I guess.   1540
WALTER: When you struck down at him from out the window?
RUPRECHT: 'Twas twice, dear Sirs.
ADAM: The scoundrel! He remembered! (*He drinks.*)
WALTER: What, twice? With two such blows you might have
    slain
The man, you know—
RUPRECHT: If I had slain him, then
I should have had him. That's just what I'd have wished.
If he lay dead before me, I could say:
'Twas he, dear Sirs, I have not lied to you.
ADAM: Yes, dead! I do believe. But thus—(*He fills a glass.*)
WALTER: Could you recognize him in the dark?
RUPRECHT: Not the least bit. How could I, gracious Sir?   1550
ADAM: Why don't you keep your eyes unbarred? Your health!
RUPRECHT: My eyes unbarred! I had them open wide.
    The devil filled them full of sand.
ADAM (*mumbling*):   Full o' sand!
    Why do you keep your big eyes open then?
    Here, gracious Sir: To what we love! Your health!
WALTER: To what is right and good and true, Judge Adam!

    (*They drink.*)

ADAM: And now the last one, if you please your Honor.

    (*He fills the glasses.*)

WALTER: You surely visit now and then, Judge Adam,
    Frau Martha's house. Now tell me, please,
    Who frequents there besides that fellow Ruprecht?   1560
ADAM: Not very often, if it please your Honor;
    And who might frequent there I cannot say.
WALTER: What? Do you not at times go visiting
    The widow of your friend deceased?

ADAM: No; for a fact it's very seldom.
WALTER: Frau Martha!
  Have you fallen out with Justice Adam here?
  He says he does not visit in your house?
FRAU MARTHA: Hm! gracious Sir, fallen out? It's not quite that
  I think he's still a good, old friend of ours,
  And yet I cannot boast that this old friend   1570
  Comes frequently to visit in our house.
  Nine weeks have passed since last he entered there,
  And then he only happened in in passing.
WALTER: What's that?
FRAU MARTHA: What's what?
WALTER: Nine weeks you say?
FRAU MARTHA: Yes, nine;
  Next Thursday will be ten. He wished to ask
  Me for some cowslip and carnation seeds.
WALTER: And—Sundays—when he goes out to his farm—?
FRAU MARTHA: Oh then, he looks in through the window then,
  And says good day to me and to my daughter too,
  And on his way proceeds immediately.   1580
WALTER (aside): Hm! Can it be I've done the man—(He drinks.)
  I thought
  Since you, at times, in your affairs have need
  To ask the maiden's service, you would show
  Your thanks, at times, by visiting her mother.
ADAM: How's that, most gracious Sir?
WALTER: How's that? You said
  The maiden helped, at times, to cure your chickens,
  The sick ones, on your farm. Did she not give
  Advice to you in this affair today?
FRAU MARTHA: Yes, to be sure, most gracious Sir, she did.
  Two days ago he sent a guinea fowl   1590
  To our house sick. Grim death had gripped its frame;
  A year ago she saved one with the pip,
  And this one too she hopes to cure by cramming.
  But he has ne'er appeared to render thanks.
WALTER (confused): Fill up, Sir Justice Adam. Do so, please.

Fill up at once. We'll have another drink.
ADAM: I'm at your service. It gives me pleasure. Here!

(*He fills the glasses.*)

WALTER: To your prosperity!—Sir Justice Adam,
Sooner or later, will surely come.
FRAU MARTHA: Think so? I doubt it.
If I could serve such Nierensteiner wine   1600
As you drink now, and which my husband, too,
The gate-keeper, had in his cellar at times,
Then would our friend, the Judge, act differently:
But I, poor widow that I am, have naught
That might allure him in my house.
WALTER: So much the better.

SCENE 11

Light and Frau Bridget, with a periwig in her hand.

The Maids. The preceding characters.

LIGHT: Here, Frau Bridget, come in.
WALTER: Is that the woman, Mr. Clerk?
LIGHT: That's she. That is Frau Bridget, please your Honor.
WALTER: So then. Let's make an end of this case now.
   Clear the table, girls.

(*The Maids carry out glasses, etc.*)

ADAM (*in the interim*): Now, Eva, listen.   1610
   You roll that pill correctly, if you please;
   Just as is right, and we shall have this evening
   A dish of finest carp out at your house.
   It must go whole right down the rascal's throat.
   If it's too large, then let him choke to death.
WALTER (*catches sight of the periwig*): What is that periwig
   which Frau Bridget

Is bringing?
LIGHT: Sir?
WALTER: What sort of wig is it that woman's
   Bringing here?
LIGHT: Hm!
WALTER: What?
LIGHT: Beg pardon—
WALTER: Well, can't I know?
LIGHT: If now your Honor will kindly
   But have our Judge interrogate this woman,   1620
   You soon will know to whom the wig belongs;
   And, without doubt, much more will be disclosed.
WALTER: I do not care to know to whom it belongs.
   How did the woman get it? Where did she find it?
LIGHT: She found the periwig high in the trellis
   Out at Frau Martha Rull's. It hung impaled
   Just like a nest among the grape-vine's tangles,
   Close by the window where the maiden sleeps.
FRAU MARTHA: At my house? In my trellis?
WALTER (secretly):   Sir Justice Adam,
   Have you aught to confide in me,   1630
   Then, please, to save the honor of this court,
   Be good enough to tell me now.
ADAM: I, in you—?
WALTER: No? Have you naught?—
ADAM: Upon my honor—

(He seizes the periwig.)

WALTER: Here, this periwig, is it not yours?
ADAM: Here, this periwig, dear Sirs, is mine!
   That is the self-same one—by Heaven and Earth!—
   Which I gave to that boy a week ago
   To bring to Master Flour down there in Utrecht.
WALTER: What? Whom?
LIGHT: To Ruprecht?
RUPRECHT: Me?
ADAM: Have I, you rascal,

ou in trust this periwig   1640
he barber to be cleaned
k ago, set out for Utrecht?
vell, yes! You gave me—
       Why didn't you then
a rascal, as you should?
you not deliver it to the master
in his workshop as I ordered you?
RECHT: Why did I not—? God—Heaven's thunder! Damn!
did deliver it into his shop.
   Master Flour took it—
         Delivered it?
And now it hangs in Frau Martha's grape-vine?   1650
Oh wait, you brat! You can't escape me thus.
It seems to me there's masquerading here.
And mutiny perhaps. Will you allow
That I at once make inquiry of this woman?
WALTER: You say you had the wig—?
ADAM: Most honored Sir,
When that young fellow there, on Tuesday last,
Drove with his father's ox-team into Utrecht,
He came into the court and said: "Judge Adam,
Have you some errands to be done in town?"
"My son," I said, "if you will be so kind,   1660
Then take this wig to town to be repaired."
I did not say: Go keep it at your house
And use it later to disguise yourself
And leave it hanging out in Martha's trellis.
FRAU BRIDGET: Dear Sirs, so please your Honor, I think 'twas not
Our Ruprecht, for when yester'en I went
Out to the farm to visit with my cousin,
Who lies quite ill with child, I heard this girl
Back in the garden scolding someone hoarsely—
Both rage and fear, it seems, stole 'way her voice: 1670
"Fie, shame on you, you low-down fellow, you,
What do you mean? Away! I'll call my mother,"
As if the Spaniards were with us again.

Then: "Eve," I cry out through the hedge,
"What's troubling you? What's up?"—The
"Well, won't you answer me?"—"What is
"What are you doing?", I ask.—"What
"Is it your Ruprecht?"—"Oh yes, of co
"So run along your way." Then go to gra
And so I thought: 'Tis but a lover's quarrel.

FRAU MARTHA: And then—?

RUPRECHT: And then?

WALTER: Hush! Let the woman fi

FRAU BRIDGET: When later I was coming from the farm
About the middle of the night, and was
Just in the linden lane by Martha's garden,
A fellow rushes past me with bald head
And with a horse-like foot; and after him
A stink like steam from pitch and hair and sulphur.
I pray a "God be with us" and then I turn
Around quite terrified, and lo! my Soul!
That pate, high Sirs, was just then disappearing,   1690
And like decaying wood lit up the lane.

RUPRECHT: What! Heavens! The deuce—!

FRAU MARTHA: Are you really mad, Frau Briggy?

RUPRECHT: You think it was the devil—?

LIGHT: Be still!

FRAU BRIDGET: My Soul!
I guess I know what I have seen and smelled.

WALTER (impatient): Woman, I will not seek to learn if 'twas
    the devil,
For against him we cannot prefer a charge.
If you can name some other person, good;
But from that sinner there you sure must spare us.

LIGHT: Will you, Your Honors, let the woman finish?

WALTER: Stupid folk, this!

FRAU BRIDGET: Good, just as you will.   1700
But Mister Light, your Clerk, can bear me witness.

WALTER: What? You, a witness?

LIGHT: To some extent, indeed.

WALTER: Forsooth, I know not—
LIGHT: Humbly I beg you
  Not to disturb the woman in her story.
  I do not dare assert it was the devil;
  But that about the horselike foot, the stink
  That followed and the baldish pate,
  Unless I err, is the whole truth.—Go on.
FRAU BRIDGET: When I today learned with astonishment
  Of what had happened at Frau Martha Rull's   1710
  And, to detect the breaker of the jug,
  Whom I that night had met there by the trellis,
  Examined close the place where he had jumped,
  I found, dear Sirs, some tracks there in the snow,
  But oh, what kind of tracks they are, dear Sirs!
  At the right, a fine and sharp and well-marked
  And real and genuine human foot,
  At the left, one lacking form, quite coarse and clumsy,
  A monster-like, a clod-like horse's foot.
WALTER (vexed): Mere gossip, foolish, insane, damnable—!   1720
VEIT: It can't be possible, woman!
FRAU MARTHA: Yes, by my faith!
  First by the trellis, where the leap took place,
  See! a wide circle trodden in the snow,
  As if a sow had wallowed 'round in it.
  And human foot and horse's foot from here,
  And human foot and horse's foot and human foot and horse's
    foot
  Right through the garden and throughout the world.
ADAM: Be damned!—Has not that rogue, perhaps, made bold,
  Disguised in devil's wise—?
RUPRECHT: What? I?
LIGHT: Hush! Hush!
FRAU BRIDGET: The hunter who seeks the badger and finds its
    tracks   1730
  Is not more jubilant than I was then.
  Your Clerkship Light, said I, for then I saw
  That worthy man come to me, sent by you,

Adjourn, adjourn the session of the court.
The breaker of the jug you cannot judge,
For he can sit in no worse place than hell.
Here is the trail which he has left behind.

WALTER: And you have thus convinced yourself?

LIGHT: Your Honor,
That which concerns the tracks is the whole truth.

WALTER: A horse's foot?

LIGHT: Foot of a human being,   1740
But *praeter propter* like a horse's hoof.

ADAM: My soul, dear Sirs, this matter seems in earnest.
So many biting words have been composed
Which would deny that any God exists;
And yet, for all I know, no Atheist
Has ever clearly proved there is no devil.
The case before us seems to be most worthy
Of special investigation. Therefore I
Propose, before we come to a conclusion,
To inquire of the Synod in the Hague   1750
Whether this court is privileged to assume
It was Beelzebub who broke this jug.

WALTER: A proposition such as you might make.
And what do you think, Clerk?

LIGHT: Your Honor will not
Have any need of synod to decide.
Complete—if it's allowed—your own account,
You, Frau Bridget, there; and this case, I hope
Out of its own connections, will be cleared.

FRAU BRIDGET: And then I said: Your Clerkship Light, let us
Trace down these tracks a little so as to see   1760
To where the devil may have made escape.
"Good," says he, "Frau Bridget, a good idea.
Perhaps we won't go so far astray,
If we go straight to Village Justice Adam."

WALTER: Well? And now you found—?

FRAU BRIDGET: Now first we found,
Beyond the garden, in the linden lane,

The place, where, letting off his sulphurous vapors,
The devil had bumped into me: a circle,
As a shy dog might yield unto a cat
When she sits down and faces him and spits.
WALTER: Then further? 1770
FRAU BRIDGET: Not far from there, there stands his monument,
Against a tree, that I must frighten 'fore it.
WALTER: A monument? What?
FRAU BRIDGET: What? Yes, there you will—
ADAM (*aside*): Be cursed, my abdomen.
LIGHT: Please, pass that by.
I beg you pass that by, Frau Bridget, please.
WALTER: I wish to know to what the tracks did lead!
FRAU BRIDGET: To what? My word! The straightest way to you,
Just as your Clerkship Light has said.
WALTER: To us? Right here?
FRAU BRIDGET: From the linden lane, indeed,
To the village green, along the old carp pond, 1780
Across the bridge, then through the cemetery,
Then, here, I say, to Village Justice Adam.
WALTER: To Village Justice Adam?
ADAM: Here to me?
FRAU BRIDGET: To you, yes.
RUPRECHT: But the devil surely can't
Dwell in the Court of Justice?
FRAU BRIDGET: In truth, I know not
If he dwells here within this house, but here
He's paid a visit, or I'm no honest woman:
His tracks lead to your threshold in the rear.
ADAM: Could he perchance have passed through here—?
FRAU BRIDGET: Yes, perhaps, passed through. May be. That's
so. 1790
The tracks out front—
WALTER: And were there tracks out front?
LIGHT: Out front, so please your Honor, there were no tracks.
FRAU BRIDGET: Oh yes, out front, the road was trodden down.
ADAM: Was trodden down. Passed through. Well I'll be damned!

That rogue has put one over on the court.
Mark that! And I'm no honest man if there
Won't be some stink when we check up the records.
If my accounts are found to be confused,
—I do not doubt they will—then on my honor,
I shall and will not vouch for anything.   1800
WALTER: Nor I.
    (*aside.*) I don't know. Was it at the left?
Or the right? I know one of his feet.
Your Honor! Your snuffbox, if you'll be so kind.
ADAM: Snuffbox?
WALTER: Snuffbox. Hand it here!
ADAM (*to Light*):   Give't to the District Judge.
WALTER: Why such ado? It only takes one step.
ADAM: It's done already. Here give it to His Honor.
WALTER: I wished to whisper something in your ear.
ADAM: Perhaps we'll have a chance a little later.—
WALTER: All right.

    (*After Light has seated himself.*)

But tell me now, dear Sirs, is there any one
In town who has ill-shaped feet?   1810
LIGHT: Hm! To be sure there's someone here in Huisum—
WALTER: So? Who?
LIGHT: Well, won't your Honor but ask our Village Judge?
WALTER: The Village Justice Adam?
ADAM: I know of none.
Ten years I've held this office here in Huisum;
For all I know there's naught but has grown straight.
WALTER (*to Light*): Whom do you mean?
FRAU MARTHA: Well you just put your feet out here!
Why do you hide them under your desk in fear,
That one 'most thinks 'twas you who made the tracks?
WALTER: Who? Your Justice Adam?
ADAM: Who? I? The tracks?
Am I the devil? Is that a horse's foot?   1820

    (*He shows his left foot.*)

WALTER: Upon my word. That foot is good.

(*Secretly.*)

Now close this session of the court at once.
ADAM: If the devil had a foot the like of that
Then he could go and dance at all the balls.
FRAU MARTHA: I say so, too. Where will the Village Judge—
ADAM: Oh what! I!
WALTER: Put an end to this at once.
FRAU BRIDGET: The only scruple which is left, dear Sirs,
  Is caused, methinks, by this grave ornament.
ADAM: What is then this grave—?
FRAU BRIDGET: Here, this periwig!
  Who ever saw the devil in such garb?
  A loftier structure and more steeped in grease
  Than a cathedral deacon wears when preaching.
ADAM: We, in this country, know but incompletely
  What is the style in Hell, our good Frau Bridget!
  They say he's wont to wear his own poor hair,
  But here on earth, I'm surely quite convinced,
  He gladly hides beneath a periwig
  To gain admission to exclusive groups.
WALTER: Oh worthless man! Worthy to be driven
  Out of this court disgraced before this people!   1840
  The honor of this court alone protects you.
  Now close this session!
ADAM: I hope that you will not—
WALTER: You hope for nothing. Retire from this case!
ADAM: Could you believe that I, the Judge, last even,
  Had left my wig there hanging in the grape-vine?
WALTER: No, God forbid! Your wig's gone up in smoke,
  Like Sodom and Gomorrah, I believe.
LIGHT: Or rather, gracious Sir, I beg your pardon,
  The cat has borne her litter in his wig.
ADAM: Dear Sirs, if now appearances condemn me,   1850
  I beg you not to act too hastily.
  To me it means either honor or disgrace.

So long as Eve is mum I fail to see
What right you have to put the blame on me.
I sit here on the Judge's bench in Huisum
And lay this wig before me on the bench,
And him who says that it belongs to me
I'll hail before the highest court in Utrecht.

LIGHT: Hm! The perwig fits you, though, my Soul!
As if it long had grown upon your scalp.   1860

(He sets the wig on him.)

ADAM: Such calumny!
LIGHT: But doesn't it?
ADAM: It's far too large
To cloak my shoulders, let alone my head.

(He looks at himself in a mirror.)

RUPRECHT: Oh such a devil-of-a-fellow!
WALTER: Quiet, you!
FRAU MARTHA: Oh such a damned, accursèd judge he is!
WALTER: Once more; will you now end this case or shall I do it?
ADAM: Yes, what is it you wish?
RUPRECHT *(to Eve)*:   Eve, speak: is't he?
WALTER: What do you mean by that, you shameless boy?
VEIT: Hush, boy, I say.
ADAM: Wait, monster, I'll get you!
RUPRECHT: Oh you damned horse-foot rogue!
WALTER: Ho there, the bailiff!
VEIT: Shut up, I say!
RUPRECHT: Wait, I'll get you today!   1870
Today you'll throw no sand into my eyes.
WALTER: Have you not sense enough, Sir Judge—?
ADAM: Yes, if your Honor
Allows then I will now pronounce the sentence.
WALTER: Good; do it. Pronounce it.
ADAM: The case has now been proven.
And Ruprecht there, the rascal, is the culprit.
WALTER: That's good. Go on.

ADAM: His neck I do condemn
  To wear the irons, and since he has made bold,
  With conduct unbecoming to his judge,
  I'll throw him into jail behind the bars.
  How long I shall determine later.   1880
EVE: My Ruprecht—?
RUPRECHT: Throw me into jail?
EVE: In irons?
WALTER: Put by your cares, my children.—Are you finished?
ADAM: The jug, I say, he may replace or not.
WALTER: 'Tis well. The session now is at an end.
  And Ruprecht will appeal to the Higher Court in Utrecht.
EVE: He shall, shall he, appeal his case in Utrecht?
RUPRECHT: What? I?
WALTER: The devil, yes! And until then—
EVE: And until then—
RUPRECHT: Shall I remain in prison?
EVE: His neck in irons? Are you a Justice, too?
  That shameless fellow there; yes, there he sits,   1890
  'Twas he himself—
WALTER: You hear? The devil! Shut up!
  Till then no one shall harm one hair—
EVE: Up, Ruprecht!
  The Justice Adam 'twas who broke the jug!
RUPRECHT: Oh, you wait!
FRAU MARTHA: He?
FRAU BRIDGET: He there?
EVE: Yes, he! Up, Ruprecht!
  He was with your Eva yesterday!
  Up! Seize him! Smite him now, just as you wish.
WALTER (stands up): Halt there! Whoever here disorder—
EVE: That's nothing!
  You've earned your irons. Go, Ruprecht!
  Go, knock him down from his high tribune there.
ADAM: Your pardon, Sirs. (Runs away.)
EVE: Here! Up!
RUPRECHT: Hold him!

EVE: Be quick!
ADAM: What?   1900
RUPRECHT: Damned lame old devil!
EVE: You get him?
RUPRECHT: Hell and damnation! No!
  It's but his cloak, not he!
WALTER: Go! Call the bailiff!
RUPRECHT (*strikes the cloak*): Rap! There's one. And rip! And
  rat! Another.
  And still another. I mean that for your back.
WALTER: You ill-bred scamp! I must have order here!
  And if you don't keep quiet now at once,
  You'll face the sentence with the irons today.
VEIT: Be calm, you wretched scoundrel, you!

SCENE 12

The preceding characters without Adam.

They all gather on the forward part of the stage.

RUPRECHT: Oh my dear Eve!
  How shamefully I've offended you today!
  Oh Heaven and Hell! Oh plague! and yesterday, too!   1910
  Oh you, my golden girl, bride of my heart!
  Can you forgive me ever in this life?
EVE (*throws herself at the feet of the District Judge*):
  If you won't help us now, Sir, we are lost!
WALTER: Are lost? And why, I pray?
RUPRECHT: Great God! What's up?
EVE: Oh save my Ruprecht from the conscript's fate!
  For this next draft, Justice Adam has confided
  To me in secret, goes to the East Indies.
  And from that place, you know, of every three
  That go, but one man comes back home alive.

WALTER: What? East Indies? Have you lost your sense?   1920
EVE: To Bantam, gracious Sir: deny it not!
　Here is the edict, a quiet, secret order,
　Concerning the militia, lately issued,
　By our own government to cover this point.
　You see, I am informed of the whole scheme.
WALTER (*takes the letter and reads it*): Oh such unheard-of
　rascally deceit! —
　That edict's false!
EVE:　　　　　　　　False?
WALTER:　　　　　　　　　　　False, as sure as fate!
　Your Clerkship Light, you tell us: Is that the order
　Which recently was sent to you from Utrecht?
LIGHT: The order! What! That sinner! Oh! A scrap   1930
　Of paper, drafted by him in his own hand! —
　The troops they now recruit are surely meant
　For service within the boundaries of this land,
　And no one thinks of sending them to the Indies.
EVE: No? Do they not, dear Sirs?
WALTER:　　　　　　　　　　　Upon my honor!
　And as a proof of this, my word, I'll buy
　Your Ruprecht free if what you say be so!
EVE (*stands up*): Oh Heavens! How that scoundrel lied to me!
　For with most frightful care he plagued my heart,
　And came when it was night to force on me   1940
　A testimonial for my Ruprecht's sake.
　He showed how falsely documented illness
　Could free him from all military service,
　Explaining and assuring thus he sneaked
　Into my room to finish the document,
　Demanding from me such disgraceful favors
　As a maiden's mouth, dear Sirs, dares not repeat!
FRAU BRIDGET: Oh, good-for-nothing, scandalous deceiver!
RUPRECHT: Come, let that horse's hoof alone, sweet child!
　Yes, had a horse destroyed that jug of yours   1950
　I'd be more jealous than I am right now.

　(*They kiss each other.*)

VEIT: I say so, too! Kiss and make up like lovers.
  Whitsunday, if you will, you may get married!
LIGHT (*at the window*): Look how our Justice Adam, I beg
  you, look,
  O'er hill and dale, as if he fled from gallows
  And rack, stamps through the ploughed-up winter-field!
WALTER: What? Is that Justice Adam?
LIGHT: Of course, it is!
SEVERAL: And now he's on the highway. Look! Just look!
  How his old wig is whipping at his back!
WALTER: Make haste, Sir Clerk, away! And bring him back!   1960
  Lest he, in mending, make the evil worse.
  Of course, I do suspend him from his office
  And place you in it, till all things are settled,
  To manage the affairs here in this village.
  If his accounts are straight, as I hope they are,
  I shall not force him to desert this place.
  Go! Be so kind, and bring him back again!

SCENE 13

The preceding characters without Light.

FRAU MARTHA: But tell me, righteous Sir, where can I find
  The seat of government in Utrecht?
WALTER: Wherefore, Frau Martha?
FRAU MARTHA (*peevishly*): Hm! Wherefore?—Don't know— 1970
  Can my jug not, perhaps, find justice there?
WALTER: Oh pardon me! Of course! On the market-place.
  And sessions are held on Tuesday and on Friday.
FRAU MARTHA: It's good! Next week will surely find me
  there.   1974

  (*All exeunt.*)

THE END